Changing the
Conversation

Changing the Conversation

THE 17 PRINCIPLES OF CONFLICT RESOLUTION

Dana Caspersen has a degree in conflict studies and mediation and works internationally as a mediator, teacher, and creator of public dialogue processes. She is an award-winning performing artist and has developed and performed choreographic work throughout the world. She lives in Germany and Vermont.

Changing the Conversation

A Joost Elffers Book

THE 17 PRINCIPLES OF **CONFLICT** RESOLUTION

Dana Caspersen

P

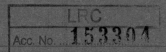
First published in Great Britain in 2015 by
PROFILE BOOKS LTD
3 Holford Yard
Bevin Way
London
WC1X 9HD

www.profilebooks.com

First published in the United States of America in 2015 by
Penguin Books

Copyright © Dana Caspersen and Joost Elffers, 2015

10   9   8   7   6   5   4   3   2   1

Set in Helvetica Neue LT Std
Printed and bound in Italy by L.E.G.O. S.p.A., Lavis (TN)

The moral right of the author has been asserted.

A CIP catalogue record for this book is available from the British Library.

ISBN 978 1 78125 4691
eISBN 978 1 78282 1693

To my parents,

with love and thanks for guiding me through many a tangle.

acknowledgments

Dana Caspersen

Thanks to everyone who has offered me their stories and helped me see possibility in conflict, to my teachers at the Woodbury Institute for their incisive, flexible wisdom, and to dancers everywhere for showing me what it means to carry out a daily practice of transformation, no matter what.

Special thanks to Joost Elffers for proposing this project and giving it form; to Carolyn Carlson, our wonderful editor at Penguin; and finally to my family, for everything.

Joost Elffers

Changing the Conversation is the result of a radical way of producing a book; there is no hierarchy in terms of content: concept, text, editing, and design are one. It is what I call a "horizontal production"—all aspects are equally important, and each part depends upon and is supported by the other.

I would like to express my thanks and appreciation to the following: Dana Caspersen for entrusting me with her writing and allowing me to visualize it; Molly Davies for introducing me to Dana; Carolyn Carlson, our editor at Penguin, for having the vision to see what this book would be. Special thanks go to Patricia Childers, an exceptional designer, who patiently and tirelessly helped me realize my design concepts for this book, and to Lindy Judge for her diligent editing and for keeping this project on track.

Conflict

You can't change how other people act in a conflict, and often you can't change your situation.

But you can change what you do.

By choosing the approaches discussed here, you can change your conversations.

► By changing your conversations,
you can resolve conflict in your life.

This book provides 17 principles for conflict resolution: practical tools for individuals in difficult situations.

*see conflict
as a moment
of opportunity*

The practice of these principles helps transform
how conflict is expressed. It offers a way to
resolve conflict from the inside, in a manner
that works for everyone involved. The principles
provide encouragement to see conflict as a
moment of opportunity. They urge us to recognize
that we have the ability to call up the curiosity
and courage needed to step away from cycles of
attack and counterattack and to move, instead,
with as much grace and skill as we can muster,
toward resolution.

Whether or not you read the chapters in this
book sequentially, I recommend taking the time
to do the exercises. The ability to engage conflict
effectively is a matter of practice. Anyone who
wants to develop this capacity can do so.

**Conflict can be both useful and inevitable.
Destructive conflict is neither.**

the anti-principles

Make Listening and Speaking Difficult

1   Hear attack. Ignore any additional information being offered.

2   Attack the other person. Create and support destructive patterns.

3   Provoke the other person's worst self.

4   Confuse needs, interests, and strategies.

5   Ignore emotions or act them out destructively.

6   Assume acknowledgment implies agreement. Don't acknowledge.

7   Make suggestions instead of listening.

8   Judge people. Try to pass your evaluations off as observations.

9   Act on your assumptions without testing them.

Ensure Stagnation or Destructive Escalation

10   Adopt a rigid stance. Don't try to understand other viewpoints.

11   Assume useful dialogue is impossible.

12   Ignore your contributions to the problem. Make things worse.

13   Pin the blame on someone. Prevent full understanding of the situation.

Prevent Positive Developments

14   Ignore conflict. Talk to the wrong people. Avoid the real problem.

15   Assume there are no good options. Settle for unsatisfying solutions.

16   Make vague agreements or no agreement at all.

17   Ignore the possibility of future conflict. Have no plans for dealing with it.

the principles

Facilitate Listening and Speaking

1 Don't hear attack. Listen for what is behind the words.

2 Resist the urge to attack. Change the conversation from the inside.

3 Talk to the other person's best self.

4 Differentiate needs, interests, and strategies.

5 Acknowledge emotions. See them as signals.

6 Differentiate between acknowledgment and agreement.

7 When listening, avoid making suggestions.

8 Differentiate between evaluation and observation.

9 Test your assumptions. Relinquish them if they prove to be false.

Change the Conversation

10 Develop curiosity in difficult situations.

11 Assume useful dialogue is possible, even when it seems unlikely.

12 If you are making things worse, stop.

13 Figure out what's happening, not whose fault it is.

Look for Ways Forward

14 Acknowledge conflict. Talk to the right people about the real problem.

15 Assume undiscovered options exist. Seek solutions people willingly support.

16 Be explicit about agreements. Be explicit when they change.

17 Expect and plan for future conflict.

facilitate listening

and speaking

My great-aunt Marie taught me that when you are knitting and the strands of yarn get tangled, it is a mistake to try to undo the knot by seeking to free only one strand.

The strands of yarn are in a complex relationship to one another. Trying to solve the problem by extracting one strand will likely increase the complexity of the knot and make it more difficult to undo.

You need to understand the complex tangle of strands before you can discover a possible solution for undoing the knot.

At first, I tried the one-strand method anyway, thinking that if I got that strand free then the rest of the knot would dissolve. Instead, I watched the knot get tighter and more complicated and finally had to pull out the scissors. At some point, I grew tired of seeing that happen and tried the method my great-aunt proposed. I started looking at the whole knot to untangle the strands.

I began to try to discover why the knot was there.

In a conflict it can be tempting to try to undo the tangle before we have a sense of why it is there and what it is composed of. We may want to see ourselves as separate from what seems to be causing us trouble: what we dislike, disagree with, or don't understand. It can be tempting to believe that by removing ourselves from those unwanted people or situations, or removing them from us, we can solve the problem.

It rarely works that way, though. We need the other people's stories to figure out what to do in a conflict. It doesn't matter whether we dislike them, distrust them, don't have faith in their reasoning capacity, or whether we love them. Their stories, in relationship to our story, tell us why the conflict is happening. The stories can help us understand what an effective solution might look like.

moving from
certainty to inquiry

Find out what is going on.

Even when you think you already understand the situation, ask the others involved what is happening with them. This doesn't mean that you need to sit through a recital of what they think you did wrong. This means ask them to tell you what they have experienced in the situation, what is important to them, and why it is important. Then, as clearly as possible and without blame, do the same.

Of course, beginning or carrying on a productive conversation can sometimes seem impossible in a difficult conflict. We might be concerned that we'll make things worse, not know what to do, or lose ground. The temptation to avoid acknowledging the conflict or to continue open hostilities once they have begun can be strong. However, we are not doomed to endlessly repeat patterns that are destructive.

We have a choice. We can engage in conflict patterns that promote damaged relationships, violence, and lost opportunities, or we can set our minds to following a different path. With attention and practice, we can develop the ability and willingness to start those difficult conversations and be present with the tangled knot of conflict in an effective and beneficial way.

We can figure out what conflict has to tell us.

Seven questions to start the conversation

Begin with the willingness to hear the other person's story and to tell yours. Whether it is in a calm conversation or something that feels more like a fight, a first step is to take a breath and shift from battling about positions to talking about experience.

It is hard to listen in a conflict. We have the tendency to rehearse what we are going to say in our minds while the other person is talking. Instead, really listen. Ask questions with the intent to understand. Here are some questions to help discover what is driving a conflict and what positive transformation might be possible from within the tangle.

Pick the questions that make the most sense for your situation and ask them of both the other person and of yourself:

1 *What is your understanding of the situation?*

2 *What is most important to you in this situation?*

3 *Why is that important?*

4 *What do you think a good outcome might look like?*

5 *What are the obstacles to reaching that outcome?*

6 *What would you like to see happen now?*

7 *Why is that important to you?*

anti-principle

Hear attack.

Ignore any additional information being offered.

principle

Don't hear attack.

**Listen for what is
behind the words.**

The principle "Don't Hear Attack" speaks to the question of perception: *What do we choose to listen for in a conflict and how do we hear what is said?*

How we listen helps determine not only what we hear and experience, but also what is possible in the situation.

Cycles of attack, defense, and counterattack often dominate the action in a conflict. This principle suggests that we step out of those cycles and change what we listen for. It suggests that we practice not hearing attack when we are being attacked. This is not naive encouragement to ignore real threat, but rather a call to change our mental stance toward the person with whom we are in conflict. "Don't Hear Attack" proposes that we listen for the real substance of the matter. Instead of hearing attack, listen for what people are really trying to say, even if they are saying it very badly.

Ask yourself:

If this were said without attack, what would it sound like?

The impulse behind this principle is not moral. It is not about being nice, ignoring your own needs, or putting yourself in a dangerous situation. Instead, it is practical. Rather than getting stuck in unproductive spirals of attack and counterattack, "Don't Hear Attack" pushes us to engage directly with what is being expressed on a level that matters and that is useful. Clearly we will notice when we are being attacked, but if we are primarily paying attention to the attack in what people say, we are wasting our time on a secondary issue. Listening past that attack requires making a choice to engage in a different action.

Focus on

hearing the "why."

Listening past attack is not easy. It often feels counter-intuitive. However, if your goal is to reduce the destructive aspects of a conflict and move toward resolution, not hearing attack is extremely effective.

Broaden your attention.

Temporarily ignore the how and what of the things being said and focus intently on the why. Do this for both yourself and the other person, even, and especially, when you are hurt or angry.

Examples of a
thought expressed
with and without
attack:

attack:

"What's the point? You never listen to me anyway."

"Immigrants are sucking up all the jobs and
draining the resources."

"If you cared about the children at this school,
you wouldn't be going on strike."

"I hate you, Mom, you never let me do anything."

"I don't want that woman in the house when you have
the kids."

no attack:

"I have something really important to tell you.
I want you to listen to me."

"I'm worried that with the current immigration policies
it will be hard for me to find a job."

"I am very concerned about how this conflict between the
school and the teachers is affecting the children."

"Mom, I need more autonomy in my life."

"I am concerned about how any new relationships we have
might affect the kids."

Consider a specific instance of attack and ask:

"What if I hadn't heard attack?

What would I have heard?"

Increasing our ability to make this translation allows real-time conflict to become less overwhelming. It makes it more likely that we can access our own capacity for listening in demanding situations. Whether in our family, workplace, community, or nation, this practice can offer us a better chance of hearing what is important, not just what is being said.

a way to
practice

Try translating this statement by
removing the attack in it:

"You're constantly undermining my
authority with the kids. Just because you
don't have the guts to follow through
on setting limits doesn't mean the kids
don't need them."

▶ **Possible translation:**

"I think the kids need to have more limits set. I worry that we are sending mixed messages, and I feel angry and frustrated when you don't support my attempts to put some limits in place."

the choice

hear attack

hear information

anti-principle

Attack the other person.

Create and support destructive patterns.

principle

**Resist the urge
to attack.**

**Change the
conversation
from the inside.**

Refusing to engage in cycles of attack and counterattack can seem foolish, possibly danger-ous, and maybe even impossible in a conflict situation.

By resisting the urge to attack, we can change the nature of the conversation we are part of, even if others continue with the attack/counterattack methodology. Destructive conflict is thwarted communication. In a conflict, people are trying to express things that are important to them. Often they express them in ineffective, confusing, and hurtful ways, which can distract everyone involved from the real topics at hand. "Re-sist the Urge to Attack" does not mean that we leave our-selves with no protection and no power. It means that we can turn the focus of the conversation away from the distraction of attack and toward what is important on a deeper level.

Speaking without attack

When you find yourself at that moment of anger or fear where the impulse to attack surges, interrupt the momentum by moving in the opposite direction. Don't attack and don't hunker down. Make the decision to do something else. Step into the uproar and disarray of conflict with the intelligence and flexibility of your heart and mind intact. Articulate what is important to you instead of attacking the other. Rather than defending your own position, try to see what has led each of you to stand where you do.

attack:

1 **You are furious that your teenage son or daughter hasn't completed a task they agreed to do.**

"What is wrong with you? How many times do I have to tell you to clean up the kitchen when you're done? I have had it with you, you're lazy and you have no respect for others."

2 **You disagree with your business partners about their hiring practices.**

"You just keep hiring miniature versions of yourselves! Don't you get it that this company needs to grow? You have no clue what it means to create an effective team. You're not choosing your next drinking buddy!"

3 **You and your siblings are in conflict about how to manage your father's estate after his death.**

"I don't understand how you can even think of selling the house. Maybe it doesn't mean anything to you, but I'm not ready to just throw away everything Dad worked for all those years. Obviously you don't get it, but family is more important than money."

no attack:

"I am so angry and disappointed that you didn't clean the kitchen after you used it. When we have an agreement, I want us to stick to it. If there is a problem with the plan, I want you to let me know."

"Let's talk about the criteria being used to hire new staff. I find the new people are too similar in skills and viewpoints to those we already have. I want this company to grow, and we need a broader palette of abilities and ideas to do it."

"I miss Dad so much. It's too much for me to think of the house disappearing, too. I understand that there are difficulties if we decide not to sell, but would you be willing to sit down with me and see if there is another option that would work for all of us?"

a way to
practice

Try filling in the blanks in the following sentence
when you find yourself in attack mode.

Use the sentence to extract the attack from
what you want to say. Then, find a way to
say it that feels natural to you.

When *(the triggering event)* happened,
I felt *(my feeling)* because *(my need/ interest)* is really important to me.

Would you be willing to *(request a do-able action)* ?

If attack creeps into
your statement, try
rephrasing it again.

For example:

1 attack

"When [you acted like your usual lazy self and didn't clean up
(evaluation of character, not description of event)], I felt [like
grounding you for the rest of the year **(strategy, not a feeling)**]
because [I need you to stop acting like a spoiled brat **(strategy
and evaluation, not a need)**]. Would you be willing [to get your
act together and grow up **(vague request)**]?"

2 attack

"When [you are irresponsible in hiring **(evaluation of character,
not description of event)**], I feel [like screaming **(strategy not a
feeling)**], because [I need you to wake up to the situation **(strategy and evaluation, not a need)**]. Would you be willing to [stop
acting like selfish idiots and think of the company for once **(evaluation and vague request)**]?"

3 attack

"When [I see you getting ready to throw away everything Dad built
(assumption about intent, not description of event), I feel
[like you just want the money **(assumption about intent, not a
feeling)**, because [you obviously don't care about family like I do
(evaluation disguised as need)]. Would you be willing to [think
about someone other than yourself **(vague request)**]?"

"When [I came home and saw the kitchen dirty], I felt [angry and disappointed] because [it's important to me that we stick to our agreements]. Would you be willing to [go over the agreements with me again and talk about what we can do to make sure this doesn't continue to happen]?"

"When [I see people being hired who are similar in skills and viewpoints to those already here], I feel [frustrated] because [I want this company to have the diversity it needs to grow]. Would you be willing to [discuss what the company needs and who might best meet those needs]?"

"When [I think of the house being sold], I feel [so sad because [I want to honor what Dad built in his life and find a way to stay connected to him]. Would you be willing to [consider if there are any other options besides selling that would work for you]?"

In order for conflict to become an opportunity, be willing to say difficult things clearly. Avoid the language of attack. Destructive conflict often seems inevitable because our habits of response are deeply ingrained.

However,

our habits

can change.

the choice

attack

inform

anti-principle

Provoke the other person's worst self.

principle

**Talk to the other
person's best self.**

Because attack and defense give rise to more attack and defense and because people tend to step up or step down to the level on which we engage them, talk to the other person's best self.

Talk to the self that can listen to and speak about what is important. Even if you suspect there is no part of the other person that would be ready or able to listen and talk in a beneficial way, try it anyway. Your willingness to give people the benefit of the doubt can turn a situation around.

For example:

addressing the less capable self:

"I don't want to talk about it because you'll just overreact again."

addressing the best self:

"Let's figure out how to talk about this. It's really important to me."

You and

the "other"

are the only
source of a
sustainable,
beneficial
outcome in
a conflict.

Conflicts don't get fixed from the outside. They may be helped by wise interventions, but ultimately the course of a conflict and its aftermath are dependent on the spirit and actions of the people involved. Assume there is a part of the other person that is capable of moving with you toward a positive resolution—and talk as if that is the case.

For example:

1

addressing the less capable self:

"Well, since you'll never follow through on an agreement anyway, I don't know what point there is to making one."

addressing the best self:

"I want to make sure that whatever we agree on really makes sense to both of us, so that it will hold."

2

addressing the less capable self:

"You're such a control freak, it's impossible to collaborate with you."

addressing the best self:

"Let's talk about how we're collaborating on this project; it feels imbalanced to me."

Whether we like it or not, we need the other person in order to untangle the conflict. Find the part of the person that you can talk to. If you can't find it, talk to it anyway. When a person's best self is addressed, that self is much more likely to emerge.

a way to
practice

Try restating this comment in a way that
would address the person's best self:

"I don't even try to bring things up
anymore, because you're incapable
of accepting feedback."

Possible restatement:

"When I have feedback for you about your work, what would be the best way for me to offer it to you?"

talk to the other person's best self

**provoke
antagonistic
dialogue**

provoke
useful
dialogue

anti-principle

**Confuse needs,
interests, and strategies.**

principle

Differentiate needs, interests, and strategies.

strategies

interests

needs

We all

have the same basic needs.

have differing interests arising from those needs.

choose different strategies to meet those needs and interests.

Needs, interests, and strategies are linked, but they are not the same thing. There are always a variety of ways to meet a need or an interest but **a strategy is an insistence on one particular path.**

Frequently, in a conflict, we can understand people's needs and interests even if we don't agree with their strategies. This understanding can make it easier to find solutions.

Every strategy is
an attempt to meet
a need or interest.

differentiate needs, interests, and strategies

Strategies

▶

Assault rifle ownership should be unrestricted.

I am going to get a job as a teacher.

I'm starting a book club.

I am apprenticing with a tailor.

I'm moving to Bangladesh.

Gay marriage should be allowed.

Interests	▶	**Needs**
I want to live in a safe neighborhood.		Safety
I want fulfilling work.		Contribution
I want to be part of a group of friends.		Community
I want to receive a good education.		Autonomy
I want new experiences.		Stimulation
I want to get married.		Intimacy

Conflicts start when the strategies we choose to try to meet our needs and interests stand in opposition to the strategies chosen by others.

My aunt Nancy, who worked in a hospital as a patient advocate, told me the story of a conflict that occurred between the family of a dying Native American man and the hospital staff.

Seen from the level of strategies, the conflict looked like this:

family's strategy:

"We need to make a fire in the hospital room."

staff's strategy:

"We cannot allow fires in the hospital."

Seen from the level of needs/interests:

family's interest:

"We want to burn some herbs as part of a ritual to help our father pass into the next world."

staff's interests:

"We want to ensure the safety of everyone in the building, and we don't want to set off any alarms."

Initially, when seen from the level of strategies, the family and the staff are in a deadlock. However, when considered from the level of needs and interests, there is motion possible.

In the hospital situation, once the needs and interests on each side became clear, the family and staff were able to negotiate a small fire in the sink of the room, which enabled the staff to ensure the safety of the situation and allowed the family to carry out the ritual to help their father prepare for death.

Sometimes we get so attached to a strategy that we bypass the need or interest underlying it. We end up fighting over strategies and positions instead of looking more broadly for effective ways to meet our needs. When this happens, we narrow the range of possibilities because we are not focusing on what is most important.

When you find things getting confusing in a conflict, stop and notice if you are engaging on the level of strategies or on the level of needs and interests.

Notice that there are a variety of ways to meet the need or interest, but an insistence on the strategy would narrow down options considerably.

Examples of strategies masquerading as needs or interests:

1

Strategy *masquerading* **as a need:**

"I need you to be home by 8:00 every night.
You're staying out too late."

Actual interest behind strategy:

"I want you to be able to get enough sleep
and do your homework."

2

Strategy *masquerading* **as a need:**

"I need a gun; this neighborhood is crazy!"

Actual need behind strategy:

"I need to feel safe."

3

Strategy *masquerading* **as a need:**

"We need to alternate evenings for cooking."

Actual interest behind strategy:

"I want more flexibility in my schedule."

But what if I don't care about the other person's needs?

Often in conflict we are not motivated to connect with the other person or persons. In that situation, it becomes even more important not to waste time arguing about strategies. To discover needs and interests you don't have to be motivated to connect; you just have to want to find a solution.

Resist the urge to keep arguing for your own preferred strategy or position. Instead, help the people you are in conflict with get a full picture of what is important to you in the situation and find out what is important to them. When the needs or interests that are driving strategies in a conflict are named, it is much more likely that a solution will be found that works for everyone involved. It is easier for people to consider alternative strategies when what is truly important to them has been acknowledged.

a way to
practice

Think back on a difficult situation that you have been in or observed.

▶ **Identify the strategies that you or others were using. Then, try to figure out which underlying needs and interests those strategies were trying to meet.**

For example:

"I need autonomy" is a **need.**

"I want reliable transportation" is an **interest.**

"I need a new car" is a **strategy.** *(A car is a form of reliable transportation that enables autonomy.)*

It can take some time to learn to make these differentiations fluidly.

Don't give up.

Once you feel a bit more comfortable looking past strategies, start trying to name your needs or interests and those of the other person when conflicts arise. Often people are not able to articulate what they need or want, and it can be helpful to guess or ask out loud what their interests or needs might be.

Be sure not to tell them what their needs and interests are, as there is a good chance that you will be wrong and that is likely to get their hackles up.

Instead, **guess** *in the form of a question.*

Use simple language like:

"So, what's the most important thing for you here?"

Is it . . .

> safety for your family?
>
> finding challenging work?
>
> having your contributions recognized?
>
> more autonomy/fun/intimacy?

Talking about needs and interests **can seem awkward at first, but don't worry too much about it.**

Sometimes people are not comfortable discussing basic needs. Talking about interests can be an easier way to enter into discussion. Interests reflect needs without the narrow focus of a strategy.

Even if you guess wrong in inquiring after the other person's needs and interests, it will shift the direction of your interaction. Although people often can't name what they need, they almost always know if you guess wrong and that alone brings you closer to understanding what is going on.

For example:

1 **"Are you wanting to quit because you need more autonomy?"**

"No, I want to be more part of the team, I feel like I'm out of the loop somehow."

2 **"So, you'd like a fence between our properties because you're looking for more privacy?"**

"No, I like talking to neighbors, I'll miss that. But I get nervous at night, I'd feel better with a fence."

3 **"We obviously have different ideas about how to organize things with the kids in the morning. What's the main thing for you? Do you want to have more of a routine?"**

"No, I guess I just don't want to be constantly negotiating. Maybe it would be better if we'd trade off getting the kids going in the morning, that way we each get a break and can make decisions on our own."

You will probably guess wrong frequently. However, as long as your intention is to discover the person's real thinking, it won't matter.

People will let you know when you get it right and, if they see you are really listening, they are much more likely, in return, to listen to you.

differentiate needs, interests, and strategies

confuse needs, interests, and strategies

differentiate needs, interests, and strategies

anti-principle

**Ignore emotions or
act them out destructively.**

principle

**Acknowledge emotions.
See them as signals.**

When my nephew
Magnus was three
years old, he told me
a story about conflict
and emotion.

The conflict in the story centered around a particularly
attractive orange cup at his preschool, which had been
allotted to a fellow classmate in spite of Magnus's interest
in it. The school had a saying to help them get through
such problems: *You get what you get and you don't get
upset.* "But sometimes," said Magnus, pulling his chin
into a deep frown, "I get upset anyway."

As Magnus points out, emotions are not optional. It is usually counterproductive to consider a conflict without considering the emotions involved. On the other hand, emotions are not the origin of conflict; they are signals of what is important to us. The intensity of our feelings allows emotion to act as an accurate signal of whether or not we are on the right track in a conflict.

However, within the complex layers of history, belief, and allegiance that shape conflict, the appearance of emotions can be bewildering. In order for emotions to help us navigate, we need to understand what is behind them.

let emotions help you see

Rather than focusing solely on emotions and letting them inform your actions in a conflict, use the emotions to help you see the system you are part of and decipher what is driving it.

Acknowledge your emotions

When you experience compelling emotions like anger, try acknowledging what you are feeling and then look behind it. Take in a deep breath of the emotion and, as you exhale, ask yourself:

"Why do I feel this way?
What do I need?"

The point here is not that we must always get what we need. The point is that in conflicts, the presence of strong emotions can either obscure what is important to us or help direct us to the heart of the matter. The challenge is to take emotion seriously, but not be swamped by its power.

Allow emotion to help initiate positive change by keeping it connected to what is important to you in the situation. Tell the other person how you feel in a way that both transmits your feeling and offers a way in, so that the person can understand what is going on with you and be a part of finding a solution.

For example:

rather than:

"Oh my God! I can't believe you dropped the ball again, you idiot! What the hell is wrong with you? I don't know how you ever got hired for this job."

try something like:

"I can't believe this! I am furious that you didn't follow through as you said you would! I worked really hard on this project, and I need this job. What is going on?"

rather than:

"This is the worst hospital staff I have ever encountered. No one will talk to me, and when they do, they're totally rude and unhelpful. It's pointless to try to ask anything because I never get any answers."

try something like:

"I'm angry about how I have been treated, I'm frustrated by the staff's lack of communication, and I'm worried about my mom. I want to talk with someone who can give me answers. Who can help me?"

Acknowledge other people's emotions

In a tense conflict, it can be easy to want to skip over talking about emotions. It can seem that their presence is obvious and doesn't need to be mentioned or that bringing attention to the emotions will make the conversation more difficult.

Even in these instances, resist the urge to dismiss people's emotions with comments like:

"Oh, grow up."

or

"That's ridiculous.
There is no reason to
feel that way."

or

"Stop complaining.
You're going to love it."

This kind of response to feelings often provokes people into circling around their emotions even harder, because the emotions remain unacknowledged. Emotions are part of our intelligent response to a situation. Acknowledge the emotion and ask what is behind it.

For example:

rather than:

"Come on, just get over it. It's not that big a deal. You're being too sensitive."

try something like:

"It sounds like you're really sad about this. What's the hardest thing about it?"

rather than:

"Would you just calm down? You're acting like a maniac."

try something like:

"It looks like you're furious about this. What's most important to you here?"

You can also offer your own emotional responses alongside the other person's as a way to look for mutual understanding.

For example:

rather than:

"Oh, now you're upset? Give me a break. If anyone should be upset here it's me. I don't even want to hear about it."

try something like:

"OK, you're angry, and I'm disappointed. What happened here? What was going on for you?"

Let the other person respond and afterward offer your own experience, saying something like:

"OK, so, here's what's going on for me . . ."

Let the other person inform you.

Because feelings are often more evident than needs, let the emotions of the other person help direct you toward understanding what is going on. If you don't understand the needs that are driving the emotions, hazard a guess. Phrase a question in a way that includes the person's emotions and focuses on asking about needs and interests.

If the person gets the sense that you are sincere in your attempt to understand, that alone can help move the conflict in a positive direction.

For example:

"Stop being so dramatic. If you don't like my boyfriend, go in your own room. He's not trying to be your dad."

"OK, it sounds like you're pretty upset about this. What's bothering you most about my boyfriend being around?"

"What are you acting all upset about? What did I do wrong now?"

"You seem frustrated. Is it because you were expecting me to do something differently?"

"Look, I don't know what your problem is, but you need to just pull it together and get the job done."

"It seems like you're having a hard time getting behind this project. Is that right?"

a way to
practice

Try reframing the response in a way that acknowledges emotions.

statement

"We never do anything fun anymore. You're always working. I feel like I never see you."

response

"I can't believe you're complaining about me working. We can't get by without the money."

Possible reframing:

"You miss us having time to just hang out together and have fun? Me too."

the choice

see emotions
as obstacles

see emotions
as helpful signals

anti-principle

Assume acknowledgment implies agreement.

Don't acknowledge.

principle

Differentiate between acknowledgment and agreement.

People have a much
easier time listening
and moving ahead
if they feel that they
have been heard.

You can acknowledge a person's position or way of thinking even when you are in complete disagreement. First, let the other person know that you are hearing him or her accurately; afterward, you can begin a discussion.

Here are some examples of simple acknowledgment:

1   **statement**

"I don't think we should take the apartment, we can't afford the rent."

response

no acknowledgment:

"It'll be fine, stop worrying all the time."

acknowledgment:

"So, you're thinking it's just too expensive for us right now?"

2   **statement**

"I don't want those kids cutting through my property."

response

no acknowledgment:

"What is your problem, you don't like kids? They're not hurting anything. It's just grass."

acknowledgment:

"OK, you don't like it when the kids cut through. Is it something they're doing while they go through, or do you just not want them on your property at all?"

Acknowledgment means letting others know you have heard their position, without adding your own approval or disapproval. The more simply you state your acknowledgment, the less likely you are to get caught up in unhelpful secondary conflicts. Acknowledge only the position, not any attack in the statement.

For example:

statement

"Nuclear power is safe. Stop being alarmist."

response

no acknowledgment:

"Alarmist? If you think that nuclear power is in the long-term interests of this state, you are insane."

acknowledgment:

"It sounds like nuclear power makes sense to you as a power source for the state."

Acknowledging viewpoints in conflict can be a way of moving past rigidly held positions. You can use the person's position as a starting point for building understanding. To do this, ask the person what it is about that position that makes it so important. Start gathering information so you can begin to understand what a sustainable resolution might look like.

For example:

statement

> "The trails should not be opened to all-terrain vehicle riders; they're all hooligans."

response

no acknowledgment:

> "It's public land, and it shouldn't be controlled by a bunch of tree-huggers. ATV riders should be able to use it, too."

acknowledgment:

> "So, you'd like to keep those roads closed to ATVs. What concerns you most about the idea of ATVs on the trails?

Differentiating between acknowledgment and agreement is a way to disentangle the opinions of others from our own responses.

For example:

Acknowledging without agreeing:

1 "It sounds like you're worried about your kids and you would feel more comfortable if the guards in the school carried guns."

2 "OK, so, you're sick of all the debris that falls onto your lawn from my tree and you're thinking cutting the tree down would be a good option?"

3 "So, it seems for you, spanking makes sense as a way to discipline kids?"

It can feel like such acknowledgment should be unnecessary because it should be obvious to the other people that we heard them, but in a conflict people often end up repeating themselves because it is, in fact, not clear to them that they were heard. Before you offer your own opinion, let others know that you heard what they said, so that they can stop trying to tell you and you can start engaging in a productive dialogue.

a way to
practice

Consider this statement and
acknowledge without agreeing.

"I don't want gay people anywhere near
my kids. They shouldn't teach or be in
the clergy."

Possible acknowledgment:

"It sounds like you feel uncomfortable about your kids
being in contact with gay
people, especially in mentor-
ing situations. Is that right?
What are your concerns?"

ignore or suppress ideas that conflict with your own

acknowledge ideas that conflict with your own

7

anti-principle

**Make suggestions
instead of listening.**

principle

**When listening,
avoid making suggestions.**

Particularly when emotions are running high in a conflict, resist the urge to jump in and start offering suggestions about what the other person needs to do.

Listen instead.

Sometimes, of course, suggestions are simply suggestions, and they can be useful. But a suggestion that is made at a point in a conflict when people don't yet feel heard will often be interpreted as a dismissal–an interruption in the telling of what is important or a lack of belief in people's ability to work things out for themselves.

Before you make a suggestion,
consider your motive for wanting to make it.

Even if we have the best intentions, making suggestions in a conflict can be unhelpful—or even harmful. Offering a suggestion can be a way of not listening, of trying to manipulate or "fix" the other person. It may be seen as a way of devaluing the needs of the other person.

Instead of trying to fix or advise the other person, ask questions to help unfold his or her story.

For example:

statement

"This whole thing is so stressful, and it's impossible to talk to you about it. You're always running off."

response

offering suggestions without listening:

1 "Look, if you would just quit that stupid job, there would be no problem."

2 "Why don't you get out of the house for once? Stop hanging around complaining."

3 "This is not my problem, OK? You need to pull yourself together. Maybe you need a therapist."

listening without making suggestions

1 "OK, what are the things you'd like to talk about?"

2 "What's the most stressful part of this for you?"

Practice

listening.

a way to
practice

Consider this scenario:

Your partner has been offered two new opportunities: a promotion in his/her current company and a job in another city. He/she wants to take the job in the other city and for you to move there as well. This would mean leaving your own job and your parents, who live close by. Your partner says that he/she has been supportive of you and now needs your support.

Try formulating some questions that will help you understand your partner's position by unfolding his or her story. Avoid letting suggestions creep in.

Possible questions:

"Sounds like you're really ready to make a change. Tell me more about the offer in the other city, what makes it especially interesting for you?"

or

"It sounds like you've been willing to live here these last years to support me, but being here hasn't really let you do what you want work-wise, is that right?"

make suggestions
without listening

listen without making suggestions

anti-principle

Judge people.

Try to pass your evaluations off as observations.

principle

Differentiate between evaluation and observation.

Observations help clarify a conflict situation.

Evaluations tend to provoke defensiveness and obscure important information being offered in a conflict. Keep the people in the conflict—both yourself and the other person—separate from the problem.

Focus on clarifying the situation.

For example:

evaluation:

1 "You are always late."

observation:

"You arrived late to our last three meetings."

evaluation:

2 "You are irresponsible. I can't trust you."

observation:

"We agreed that you would be home by 10:00, and it is now 11:00."

evaluation:

3 "This company has sexist policies."

observation:

"There are only two women in the upper-level management of this company."

evaluation:

4 "You are a jerk."

observation:

"You interrupted me every time I tried to speak."

Avoid telling people what they "are."

Instead, describe how their actions affect you.

Resist the urge to make evaluations of the other person's intent or character. Even if you believe your evaluation is valid, such comments usually ratchet up the tension without increasing understanding.

Instead, describe what you have observed or experienced. Find a way to articulate why the situation has you riled up. Take the energy of your anger and redirect it into accurately describing how the other person's actions have affected you and why.

By not pinning the other person down with accusation, blame, or labeling, you leave space for both of you to maneuver into a solution-seeking mind-set instead of a mind-set of attack or defense.

For example:

1

"You're such a bitch. You constantly try to undermine me."

observation and experience:

"You came in and yelled at me in front of everyone this morning. I hate that. If there is a problem, let me know in private."

2

evaluation:

"You wouldn't know a work ethic if it bit you in the ass. You're lucky to be here, but obviously you don't get that."

observation and experience:

"Of the five projects that you agreed to complete, only one is finished. I took a chance hiring you. This is not what I expected."

3

evaluation:

"I don't know why I trusted you in the first place. You're totally irresponsible. You can forget about going out tomorrow night."

observation and experience:

"When you didn't come home on time, I was worried about you and angry that you didn't hold up your end of the bargain."

a way to
practice

Try reframing this evaluation as a statement of observation and experience.

"Obviously you're too self-absorbed to notice, but other people in this building have to work and are not interested in listening to you blasting your music night and day."

Possible reframing:

"I have to get up at 5:00 a.m. for work. Every night this week there has been music playing in your apartment until 1:00 a.m., and it has been keeping me awake. I am exhausted from not sleeping. I would like to make an agreement with you about when music is played."

offer evaluation

offer observation and experience

anti-principle

Act on your assumptions without testing them.

principle

Test your assumptions.

Relinquish them if they prove to be false.

"Thus waking consciousness is dreaming—but dreaming constrained by external reality."

—Oliver Sacks

An Anthropologist on Mars: Seven Paradoxical Tales

My cousin's daughters were tucked up close, listening to me read a story about fairies. The story took a sudden turn that I hadn't anticipated, where the fairies led away children who had lied and drowned them in a swamp. "Is that true?" said Emily, drawing her eyebrows together. "I hope not."

We live on stories. We thrive, fail, create, adapt, and connect through our minds' capacity to synthesize disparate pieces of information into a coherent whole. But as Emily points out, some stories are not true and some that we wish weren't true, are. We don't know which is which until we investigate. But in conflict, we often stop investigating and start assuming, and so the stories we tell ourselves are built on static, one-sided information.

We often assume that we understand another person's feelings, intentions, and character. Frequently we act based on our assumptions, and often we strengthen our assumptions by listening selectively—choosing to pay attention only to information that supports our beliefs.

Very often, however,

our assumptions are wrong.

Relying on assumptions often decreases understanding and obscures productive ways forward. Try something else instead. Consider your assumptions and how they are shaping your response to the other person. To avoid unnecessary confusion and suffering, don't rely on your assumptions: test them.

Find out what is really happening.

If you discover that your assumptions are false, let them go.

Ask simple questions like:

1 "It looks to me like you're not comfortable hiring a woman for this position. Is that right?"

2 "I'm guessing that your primary interest is getting the repairs done with a minimum of cost. Is that correct?"

3 "I'm assuming the reason you don't want to discuss this is because you disagree with me, is that the case?"

a way to
practice

Consider this statement and recast it as a
question that tests assumptions:

"You obviously think this project is a
waste of time and you are determined
to sabotage it."

► **Possible recasting:**

"I have the sense that
you think this project is
not worth working on.
Is that true?"

the choice

**assume
you are right**

test your
assumptions

change the

conversation

One summer, I tried to move a large mound of tangled tree stumps and dirt that had been bulldozed onto a trail I was clearing through the woods. In the process, I discovered two things. First, cutting off the visible tree branches and roots sticking out of the dirt does not make the mound any less tangled. Second, trying to yank a tree out of the dirt without understanding what you are pulling and what it is connected to is a waste of energy. Eventually, after proving to myself through repeated efforts that those methods weren't getting me anywhere, I paused.

I began to look at the tangle of stumps and dirt differently.

I realized that the branches and roots sticking up out of the earth were the pathway to a tangle that I could not see. By following them down into the dirt, I could reach the heart of the knot much more easily than blindly digging away at the hundreds of pounds of earth on top. As I worked, I found that the roots and branches were actually holding the mound together. Once I freed them, the tree stumps rolled out with relative ease.

Often in conflict, the tangled mechanics of the situation are similarly obscured. As a result, it can be tempting to try to get rid of the visible signs of conflict and pretend it is not happening, or to force through our own strategies without understanding the true shape of the situation. However, the tactics of avoidance or force combined with ignorance usually produce either simmering or escalating conflict—and leave the root causes undiscovered.

Right at the moment when we feel like shutting down and focusing on getting our own way or proving the other person wrong, we can instead illuminate the tangle under the dirt by shifting our mental stance from one of certainty to one of inquiry. If we look with curiosity on what seems most difficult, it will eventually yield up the workings of the tensions that are holding the situation in place.

anti-principle

Adopt a rigid stance.

Don't try to understand other viewpoints.

principle

Develop curiosity in difficult situations.

The ability to *remain* curious in difficult situations is a skill. It takes practice. It is the ability, in the presence of anger and fear, to continue to ask:

**"What is really going on here?
What have I not yet understood?"**

Robust, persistent curiosity is transformative. It enables us to see possibility from within conflict. However, in the tension of conflict, our first impulse is often to abandon curiosity. When this happens, we stop trying to understand the other people. We become more willing to see them get hurt and are less able to see ourselves as being in relationship to them. To varying degrees, we begin to dehumanize the other people. We move away.

But we can adopt a mental stance of persistent, intelligent curiosity toward situations and people—even if we are not curious about them. This is not a suggestion to step into harm's way or to pretend closeness where there is none. "Develop Curiosity in Difficult Situations" suggests that we persist in wanting to know as much as possible about the larger story in a conflict, not just what is evident from our own point of view. This principle is a push to figure out what it takes to develop a real willingness and ability to be present with what we dislike, fear, or disagree with, and still be capable of listening for what we have not yet heard.

For example:

No Curiosity:

1   I want him to just shut the hell up.

2   They are such idiots, they don't care what happens to the country.

3   If she was gone, everything would be fine.

4   It is a waste of time to talk to him, he's impossible.

5   What is wrong with her? How could she do that to me?

6   She/he needs to (…fill in the blank…).

Curiosity:

1 What is he is actually trying to say?

2 What is important to them and why?
How does this make sense to them?

3 What have I not yet noticed about this situation?
What are my decisions to make?

4 What is the main obstacle in our conversation right now?
Why is it there?

5 What led her to take that action?
What did she need?

6 What can I do differently?

**a way to
practice**

Think about a conflict that you are familiar
with at home, at work, or out in the world.

Pick one that really pushes your buttons.

Start gently and, as you think it through,
notice how and when you lose curiosity
about the other person.

Notice how you close down: what happens
in your body, your thoughts, and your
emotions. Instead of pushing those reactions
away, become knowledgeable about them.
Breathe them in, and each time you exhale,
imagine the space around you easing up.

To wake your curiosity back up, ask yourself the following questions:

1. *How does what this person thinks make sense to him or her?*

2. *What has led this person to take these actions?*

3. *At the heart of it, what does this person want or need?*

4. *Am I contributing to the difficulty of the situation?*

5. *What needs to change in order for a useful dialogue to take place?*

Notice when you are tempted to answer with something like, "Because (s)he's a jerk," and resist that urge. Instead, take a breath, exhale, and choose a curious mind-set.

develop curiosity in difficult situations

abandon your curious mind

strengthen your curious mind

principle 11

anti-principle

Assume useful dialogue is impossible.

principle

Assume useful dialogue is possible, even when it seems unlikely.

We are capable of
engaging in useful
dialogue even in the
worst situations.

Even when we make countless mistakes and missteps along
the way, we can develop the ability to right ourselves and
choose a path that leads to where we want to go. "Assume
Useful Dialogue Is Possible" is not an exhortation to ignore
reality and engage in wishful thinking. Rather, it is a prompt
to question the rigidity of our own beliefs and the scope of
our understanding.

Consider what is blocking useful dialogue in the conflict.
Given the people involved and their needs, think about what
concrete changes might make dialogue possible.

When forward motion seems blocked, think about which steps you might take to create useful dialogue.

Block: **Unclear roles**

Steps to take: **Establish which decisions need to be made and who is responsible for making them.**

Clarify roles to better focus your dialogue. Clarify who is responsible for making which decisions. If the decision is yours to make, take responsibility and make it; don't blame other people for the continuing uncertainty. If the decision is not yours to make, leave it in the hands of those responsible. Be clear about your reaction to their decisions rather than trying to control what they decide. If you feel that roles should change, make that an explicit topic of discussion.

For example:

If a friend has been staying with you for several months, you can request that s/he start paying rent, but whether or not your friend's share of the rent is paid is your friend's decision. Your decision is what you do in response. It is important to recognize the responsibility and the right that each person has. Acknowledging that each person must make his or her own decisions is a gesture of respect that can both clarify and ease difficult situations.

Block: People won't budge

Steps to take: **Shift the conversation from strategies to needs.**

If you are stuck on strategies or positions, shift the focus to needs. Take a step back and check that you have understood what is important to the other person. Make sure that you have made your own interests clear as well. If you find yourself clinging tight to a particular position or strategy, loosen your grasp for a moment and change your approach to a more investigatory one. Positions tend to solidify under scrutiny, while conversations about interests tend to create movement.

Try asking something like:

"Can you talk some more about your specific concerns re-garding the proposal to build a drug treatment center in the neighborhood?"

or

"So, it sounds like the idea of my new partner sleeping over when I have the kids is really not sitting well with you. What are you most concerned about?"

Block: **Conflicting beliefs**

Steps to take: **Open a broader dialogue.**

In conflicts that take place in an atmosphere of strongly held beliefs, orient the conversation away from arguing about the beliefs themselves. Broaden the conversation by asking about people's experiences and how those experiences have shaped their beliefs.

For example:

1 "There are so many issues involved when we start talking about what kind of education we want for our kids. What's at the heart of it for you?"

2 "It sounds like you're concerned that changing the zoning to allow more rentals could be bad for the neighborhood. Would you talk more about how your experience has shaped your thinking on this?"

3 "So, we've got some different ideas about how much we should be saving for the future. What are your thoughts about how we should prioritize when it comes to finances?"

Block: Group identity defined by conflict

Steps to take: **Differentiate allegiances from the conflict; encourage curiosity.**

Sometimes conflicts remain in place because the conflict is part of the identity of a group. Groups build boundaries between "them" and "us." Particularly in a long-standing conflict, concern can arise that others might see motion toward resolution as a form of betrayal.

Ways to create positive motion:

Talk openly about the issue if possible. Discuss the potential damaging results of not being willing to engage in dialogue with the other side. Acknowledge as well the bonds that are important within each group and differentiate the bonds from the conflict.

Try something like this:

"This is an important issue for us. In some ways it defines who we are as a group. For some of us, moving toward dialogue with the other side might feel like a betrayal of our position. I understand the desire to remain strong on our goals. At the same time, in order to find a solution, we need to be willing to talk with the people on the other side of this issue. Not having that dialogue could be damaging for us in the long run. I'd like to be sure the people on the other side understand why we stand where we do on the issues. I'd also like to get a better sense of what they're thinking—and why.

How does that sound? What can we do to make that dialogue possible?"

Block: Threat of loss of face

Steps to take: **Create an environment that allows for changing directions.**

Often people need reassurance that if they shift directions or back away from positions, they will still be respected and seen as credible. Focus on finding a pathway to resolution that doesn't leave anyone embarrassed or with a lingering urge to even the score. Avoid personal attacks.

To help create an atmosphere where people feel free to let go of one strategy and look for others, focus on the characteristics of the strategy under discussion–what it allows for or prevents–rather than the strategy as a whole. Make sure the other people know that you understand the reasons behind their interest in that strategy. Name those interests as valid and important information for finding a solution that will work.

For example:

statement

"If I don't get an assistant, there is no way I can take care of all these new clients."

non face-saving:

"Oh, you want an assistant? Yeah, right, get in line. You think you're the only person here with too much work? When we have money to throw around, I'll let you know."

response

face-saving:

"I agree, spending time with new clients is a priority. What's another way to do that without hiring a new assistant? We don't have the budget for that."

Block: **Lingering mistrust**

Steps to take: **Build verifiable assurances into agreements.**

If there is a substantial amount of mistrust between the people who are in conflict, talk explicitly about how to build verifiable assurances into any agreement.

In a more formal situation try something like:

> "It seems like we all want assurances that what we agree to here today will be upheld. Let's write down the concerns that people have about maintaining the agreement and build some assurances into the agreement itself."

In a more personal situation try something like:

> "It sounds like you're thinking that what we agree to might not actually happen. Is that right? Let's talk about where things still feel uncertain and what we can do so we both feel secure about it."

assume useful dialogue is possible

Consider what might make useful dialogue possible.

Ask yourself the following questions:

1 *"Am I willing to engage in a useful dialogue? Is the other person willing?"*

2 *"If not, what would need to change in order for each of us to become willing?"*

3 *"What is making it difficult for us to talk in a productive manner?"*

4 *"What concrete changes could make a useful dialogue possible?"*

Exclude answers that involve other people changing their personalities.

assume useful dialogue is possible

ignore
the possibility of
useful dialogue

pursue the possibility of useful dialogue

anti-principle

**Ignore your
contributions to
the problem.**

Make things worse.

principle

**If you are making
things worse, stop.**

Part of a Buddhist prayer reads: *"Revulsion is the foot of meditation."* It suggests that finally growing sick and tired of our unhelpful habits will help us bring about change.

Because changing our habits in conflict takes substantial effort, we not only have to be sick of the way things have been going, but we also need to make a decision to change and then be prepared to act on that decision.

Sometimes our reaction to conflict is so ingrained that it seems impossible to change. However, the way we approach and engage with conflict is not a fundamental part of our character, it is a learned behavior. We can change it.

Consider your primary goal in the conflict: What are your underlying needs and interests? Ask yourself if your actions are in line with your goals. If they are not, choose different actions.

For example:

In a conflict between a mother and a teenage child about getting up for school, compare the mother's statements/actions with her primary goal:

Mother's primary goal:

> A morning routine that provides a relaxed beginning to the day and allows everyone to get where they're going on time.

Her statements/ actions:

> "Would you just get up? Stop acting like a five-year-old! I am so sick of this, you are driving me crazy!" **(attacking and blaming).**

Likely outcome:

> The conflict is now worse. The child is angry and defensive and launches into a counterattack. No solutions have been found, and the likelihood of leaving on time is lower than before.

Sometimes our unhelpful actions feel temporarily satisfying, so it can be harder to take the obvious step of abandoning those actions. Try naming them and consciously choosing alternatives. Take a look through the list of anti-principles at the beginning of this book; if your actions are in alignment with any of them, take a step back and shift directions.

In this conflict, once the mother notices that she has chosen actions that include blame and attack, she can change the conversation by consciously changing her approach. She can stop attacking and blaming and instead do the opposite: inquire, listen to and state needs, look for possibility.

For example:

"So, it looks like it's tough for you to get up for school on time, right? Let's talk about what could make that easier. I want our mornings to start in a good way. What are some of the things that make it harder for you to get up? What are some things that we could change that would help? What can I do? What can you do?"

We can change what we do in conflict. This may seem like a daunting endeavor, but it can be taken one small step at a time. The process of changing habits is not a single event but a series of decisions that we undertake daily as we decide how to listen to and engage with the world. Over and over, we can decide to stop doing one thing and start doing another.

if you are making things worse, stop

We can change

what we do.

a way to
practice

Consider your actions and inactions
in the conflict.

Ask yourself:

1 *"Am I preventing constructive dialogue or causing the conflict to escalate in a destructive way?"*

2 *"Am I sabotaging a potentially valuable agreement?"*

3 *"Am I avoiding important but difficult conversations or creating division instead of connection?"*

4 *"Are my actions in line with my goal?"*

**inhabit conflict
destructively**

inhabit conflict constructively

anti-principle

**Pin the blame
on someone.**

**Prevent full understanding
of the situation.**

principle

Figure out what's happening, not whose fault it is.

Establishing blame and acknowledging the contributions that each person has made to the problem are two different things.

Blaming obscures the mechanics of the conflict and keeps the focus on the past. It distracts us from finding out what happened and why, and makes it much more difficult for people to talk constructively about difficult things.

Looking at contributions, however, illuminates the mechanics of conflict in a way that orients our focus toward the future and toward functional solutions. This can be accomplished even with people who prefer adversarial interactions.

For example:

Mini-version of a blame conversation:

statement

"That meeting was a disaster, and it's your fault. You can never keep your damn mouth shut."

response

"What, no one should talk except you? The problem is you don't know how to run a meeting."

statement

"You make it impossible to run a meeting when you're constantly shouting at everyone!"

response

"Those meetings are a waste of time anyway."

statement

"No, it's a waste of time because you're acting like a jerk."

response

"Fine, you go ahead and run those meetings without me."

Mini-version of a conversation about contribution:

statement

> "I was really frustrated with how that meeting went, and it seemed like you were, too."

response

> "Yeah, a total waste of time, as usual."

statement

> "I think part of it was that I didn't schedule enough time for people to talk. I also think the way you approached them was really pushing their buttons."

response

> "Well, yeah, you never let anyone have a chance to speak, and then we all end up just shouting to get our point across."

statement

> "OK, so let's talk about what we can change next time. I'll make sure people have a chance to speak, and I think we need some communication ground rules for when it gets tense. What do you think?"

response

> "I think if I am coming to another meeting, it definitely needs to be different."

statement

> "All right, let's sit down and figure it out."

Acknowledge your own contributions.

For example:

"Look, I think I've been making this whole thing worse by trying to micro-manage everyone. I'm going to try to step back some."

If one person moves away from blame and toward problem-solving, the attention of the conversation as a whole tends to shift. People are more willing to talk about their contributions to the problem if it is clear that the point of doing so is to offer information toward creating a solution that meets their needs and not toward finding a target for blame.

Acknowledge the other person's contributions.

Acknowledging your own contributions doesn't mean ignoring the contributions of the other person. On the contrary, if you avoid bringing the contributions of the other to light, you misrepresent the situation and deprive the other person of the chance to be part of transforming it in a positive way. Be explicit about your observations and thoughts regarding the other's actions and let them know what you would like to see change and why. Do so without attack and blame.

For example:

1

blaming the other:

"It's your fault. If you wouldn't scream at me right when I get home, I wouldn't lose it. You should know better. I'm always tired when I get home from work."

acknowledging the other's contribution:

"When you start talking about problems right when I get home from work, I have a hard time reacting well. I need 10 minutes to unwind first. OK?"

2

blaming the other:

"I can't get my ideas out because you never let me talk. It's always about you. You don't listen to anyone else."

acknowledging the other's contribution:

"You shot down my ideas before I could explain them. I lost my nerve and didn't try again. I'd like you to hear me out."

a way to
practice

Recast this statement without blame.

"Do you have any idea how hard I work to pay for that school? I have no life because of you, and you've wasted my time and money partying with your friends."

► **Possible recasting:**

"You have been skipping classes and your grades have dropped. It is important to me that you have a good education, and I have worked hard to make that possible. I am angry that you have not applied yourself to your studies. What is going on?"

the choice

blame the other

figure out what happened

look for ways

forward

I once tried to lay a new trail in the forest from one known point to another, through woods that were dense and terrain that was unpredictable. I began at the first point and moved through, leaving markers as I went, but became sidetracked by fallen trees and unexpected streams and lost my way in the brush, unable to find a path to the other point. I then tried the same thing from the second point, hoping that I would run into my first trail, but the woods looked different from each new angle, and I couldn't find the connection.

One day, I tried a different tactic.

I stood at the first point, my husband Bill stood at the second, and we called across to each other. Moving toward each other's voices, we made our way through the landscape, marking a trail as we went, until we were able to join the paths we were creating.

Motion toward resolution in conflict requires clarity about the point where we each begin, an awareness of the environment through which we move, and curiosity about what is needed to make that movement possible. The voices calling out from both sides of a conflict help us find our way through its convoluted landscapes, even if those voices are unwelcome. A trail is built on the terrain that is present and enables passage in both directions. In order to navigate that terrain well, we need the vantage point from each side to understand the dangers and obstacles as well as the possibilities and challenges. This last group of principles offers thoughts on how we can begin to carry out the actions that can lead to resolutions that work and that last.

anti-principle

Ignore conflict.
Talk to the wrong people.
Avoid the real problem.

principle

Acknowledge conflict.

Talk to the right people about the real problem.

When conflict is addressed, it brings issues to light and can motivate people to engage in challenging conversations. When it is not addressed, conflict tends to fester and either escalate or become a chronic source of frustration, stress, and pain.

We often avoid addressing the real problem in conflict, and we frequently do this by avoiding talking to the people we are in conflict with about our concerns. Instead, figure out with whom you are really having the problem and talk to them directly. Avoid the temptation to try to address the problem by ranting about the situation in general, complaining behind people's backs, or attacking them in indirect ways. Name the problem instead. Describe the issue under discussion in terms that everyone can accept by describing the issue itself, not your current preferred outcome or evaluation of the other person.

For example:

1 **rather than:**

"The problem here is that you don't know how to be a parent. You let the kids get away with everything."

try:

"It seems to me that the main issue here is how we are going to respond when the kids act out. Is that how you see it?"

2 **rather than:**

"I should just quit. You obviously don't respect or appreciate my work, and you take all the credit anyway."

try:

"I'd like to talk about how we credit our collaborative work. Currently, I don't think it reflects each of our contributions."

Make specific, do-able requests.

Once the problem has been named, identify your needs or interests, and then make a specific, do-able request. Don't be attached to the specific strategy that you suggest; stay focused on the underlying needs. The other person may not agree with the strategy you propose, but making a request instead of attacking, evaluating, or avoiding the other person can help get the conversation going in a productive direction.

For example:

1

"Stop driving like a maniac. You're going to get us killed."

try something like:

"I get nervous when you drive this fast. Would you be willing to stay under 70 mph?"

2
rather than:

"You are so lazy and irresponsible. You're taking advantage of me. You've been out of college for a year. Do you think I'm going to keep paying for everything forever?"

try something like:

"I want us to have a fair financial arrangement. Would you be willing to start contributing money toward household costs each month?"

When it is clear what is important to each person in the situation and what s/he is willing to do as a result, it's easier to understand which decisions are yours to make and to make those decisions consciously.

Separate issues

If you find yourself in a conflict where there are many issues, try making a list and talking about the issues one at a time. Acknowledge the connection between the issues while keeping the main questions in the foreground.

For example:

1 "It seems like the main question here is how salary levels are decided. At the same time, it sounds like the question of communication between departments is also important to you, and maybe we need to talk about that first. Is that how you see it?"

2 "I think the main issue here is how we divide household tasks. It sounds like we are also disagreeing about how clean we should keep the apartment. Should we talk about who does what first and then figure out a level of cleanliness that we can both agree on?"

a way to
practice

Try reframing the following statements:

1 "You are hopeless with money, and your spending is out of control. I want to be in charge of the household finances from now on."

Reframe by naming the issue, without including your preferred strategy or an evaluation of the other person.

2 "You're so patronizing when we are talking to our accountant. Stop treating me like an idiot. Just because I don't talk nonstop like you doesn't mean I don't understand what's going on."

Reframe as a specific, do-able request.

► Possible reframing:

1 "I want to talk about how our household money is spent. I don't agree with the way you have been using the funds."

2 "If there is something that I don't understand, I will ask. If I'm quiet, it's because I'm thinking. Please wait for me to ask before you start re-explaining things to me."

the choice

keep the
problem undefined

define the problem

anti-principle

Assume there are no good options.

Settle for unsatisfying solutions.

principle

Assume undiscovered options exist.

Seek solutions people willingly support.

Successful solutions
meet people's needs.

This doesn't mean that all needs must be met. It means
that if you want a solution to last, it must satisfy everyone
involved to some degree. Be sure that you and the other
person/people have reasons to stick to any agreement that
is made.

Don't rush into finding a solution. Hold in your mind the
possibility that options might exist that have not yet been
discovered, options that may do a much better job of meeting the needs of the people involved. To allow new ideas to
emerge, acknowledge the strategies that come up simply as
options, not as final solutions that you need to either defend
or reject. Use the options that are offered as a way of finding
out what is important to everyone.

For example:

In a dialogue on urban chicken farming:

idea/strategy offered:

"The council should adopt an ordinance to ban raising chickens in the city."

acknowledgment:

"OK, so one option is to completely ban chickens within the city limits."

uncovering interests:

"What specific things would banning chickens help with? What would it prevent or make possible?"

Find out what needs the solution must meet.

To provoke ideas that could result in beneficial solutions, look at what each person in the conflict wants. Pose questions that ask how those different needs and interests can be held together.

listen for what you have not yet heard

For example:

Consider a conflict about playing time in a competitive youth soccer team where the interests are:

parent

"Youth sports should strive to teach kids how to be good human beings. I want players to be rewarded for hard work and given field time, regardless of their skill level."

coach

"This a competitive team and skill is paramount. The players who can help us win should have the most field time, regardless of their attitude toward practice."

> **rather than asking:**

"Who should get field time?"

> **ask:**

"What would it look like if the team valued both excellence and hard work? How could that be reflected in the way playing time is distributed?"

Ideas for effective solutions come from considering the needs on all sides of a conflict. To find a solution that addresses those needs, listen for what you haven't heard yet, not what you already know.

a way to practice

Consider this conflict and ask a question to bring undiscovered options to light.

father
"You obviously can't keep up with your schoolwork and play varsity basketball at the same time. I'm taking you off the team."

daughter
"I am not quitting the basketball team, Dad. I don't care about grades, I'm probably not going to college anyway."

▶ **Possible question:**

"What would it look like
if it worked to play on
the team and have a B
average at the same time?
What changes might
make that possible?"

**assume all
options are known**

be curious about undiscovered options

principle 16

anti-principle

Make vague agreements or no agreement at all.

principle

Be explicit about agreements.

Be explicit when they change.

When you have come
to a resolution, make
sure everyone is agree-
ing to the same thing.

Explicitly name all aspects of what you have agreed to. Don't
assume that is clear to everyone. Often it is not clear. Particularly when you are dealing with the aspects of the conflict
that are most difficult to talk about.

Although it can be tempting to just be glad that you reached some kind of agreement and let the fuzzy areas slide, doing so often results in problems later. It is worthwhile to test the agreement to see where it might fall apart—with the intention of making it as robust and suited to the needs of the situation as possible. While it can feel uncomfortable to go wading back into areas that have been inflammatory, naming the difficult areas explicitly without using blame or attack can help to defuse the tension around them. It can normalize the idea that it is possible to talk about difficult topics without negative repercussions.

Clarify expectations

Once you have come to a solution about how to move forward and people have taken a moment to exhale, introduce the idea of testing the solution. Call up your curiosity and use simple language.

For example:

"I'd like to go through this one last time to make sure we are in agreement on all of the points."

Go through what you have agreed to step by step. If you come to an area that you suspect is unclear, say something like:

"So, this is an area that has been tense and somewhat difficult to talk about. I'd like to double-check here, to make sure that what we're agreeing to now is clear and really makes sense to everyone."

"So, let's just go over this one more time to make sure it's clear, OK?"

Offer your understanding of what you have agreed to. To check about tricky aspects, try saying something like:

"It seems like this was the hardest part to talk about. I want to double-check to make sure we both feel OK about what we came up with. How are you feeling about this?"

Over time the

situation may change,

and it may be necessary to alter your agreement or find a different solution. When that occurs, bring the subject up explicitly. Check to be sure that any changes to the agreement are mutually acceptable and understood. Don't rely on assumptions.

Help create a situation where people have a sense of clarity, freedom, and security by defining what is and is not contained within your agreement.

a way to
practice

Consider this scenario and find a way to test the agreement:

You share a car with a friend and you have had conflict regarding the schedule for using the car. You have talked it through and come up with an agreement about which days each person uses it, but there is no plan covering unexpected situations.

Possible way to test the agreement:

"I think the schedule for when we use the car is clear now. I use it Monday and Thursday, all day, and you have it the rest of the time. Right? OK, good.

"So, let's talk about how we handle it if something unexpected comes up and one of us wants to use it on a different day."

make vague agreements

make clear agreements

anti-principle

Ignore the possibility of future conflict.

Have no plans for dealing with it.

principle

**Expect and plan for
future conflict.**

After you make your way through a conflict, talk openly about how you will handle problems that arise in the future.

It can be tempting to think of conflict as an aberration, but it's not. Conflict is continual. It is the friction that results from the constant overlapping, weaving, and striking together that takes place between our own story and the story of the world. Speaking openly about strategies for addressing future conflict helps prevent unnecessary escalation and destructive outcomes.

Practice welcoming the information and impetus that conflict provides. Make it more possible to access that energy and information in a constructive way by planning for how to talk during future times of friction. As part of working out a resolution, talk about what happens if the agreement fails or the situation changes.

To introduce the idea, use simple language like:

"I'm glad that we found a way to work this out and that we're able to discuss these difficult issues. I'd like to think about what we will do in the future if other issues come up. Maybe we can make a plan for how we will bring up any problems that we see and how we could best talk with each other about it. How does that sound to you?"

Talk explicitly about how you will raise issues. Find out what helps each of you react best in conflict and develop strategies for how you will communicate with each other when problems arise.

It may seem that anticipating future conflicts could exacerbate tensions that already exist. On the contrary, naming the likely possibility of future conflict and developing a mutual plan for how to handle it places conflict in a context where it can be seen as a normal, potentially productive part of our lives. It creates a basis for ongoing, beneficial connection in difficult times.

1 "It is easier for me if you bring problems up in private, not in front of the others."

2 "I have a hard time listening if you yell at me. Can you wait until you can say it without yelling? Just say something like 'not now,' so that I know what's happening."

3 "How about if we make a hand signal or something, so we can let each other know when we are getting tense?"

4 "I would prefer to keep things formal. How about if we choose representatives who will call a meeting if a problem arises?"

5 "If you start feeling a problem is coming up, please let me know right away—even if it seems like a bad time, I want to know."

a way to
practice

Consider this scenario and start a conversation about handling future conflict.

There has been tension in your neighborhood between shopkeepers and a group of young people who like to hang out on the street. You and the other young people met with the store owners and came to an agreement about what kind of activities will happen in front of the shops. You think things might get tense again, though, if a new problem comes up. You don't want the police to be involved again.

▶ **Possible way to start the conversation:**

"OK, it seems like this is a good plan for now. Let's figure out what we will do if another problem comes up, though, so we can try to work it out together without the police. How does that sound?

"What would make it easier for us to communicate on issues in the future?"

ignore the possibility of future conflict

plan for
future conflict

Conflict is a place of possibility.